T0130764

the book of grief
and hamburgers

SELECTED OTHER BOOKS BY STUART ROSS

70 Kippers (w/ Michael Dennis, Proper Tales Press, 2020)

Ninety Tiny Poems (above/ground press, 2019)

Sos una Sola Persona (trans. Tomás Downey & Sarah Moses, Socios Fundadores, 2019)

Motel of the Opposable Thumbs (Anvil Press, 2019)

Espesantes (above/ground press, 2018)

Eleven/Elleve/Alive (w/ Dag T. Straumsvåg & Hugh Thomas, shreeking violet press, 2018)

Pockets (ECW Press, 2017)

A Sparrow Came Down Resplendent (Wolsak and Wynn, 2016)

Sonnets (w/ Richard Huttel, serif of nottingham editions, 2016)

A Hamburger in a Gallery (DC Books, 2015)

Further Confessions of a Small-Press Racketeer (Anvil Press, 2015)

In In My Dreams (Book*hug, 2014)

Our Days in Vaudeville (w/ 29 collaborators, Mansfield Press, 2013)

You Exist. Details Follow. (Anvil Press, 2012)

Snowball, Dragonfly, Jew (ECW Press, 2011)

Buying Cigarettes for the Dog (Freehand Books, 2009)

Dead Cars in Managua (DC Books, 2008)

I Cut My Finger (Anvil Press, 2007)

Confessions of a Small-Press Racketeer (Anvil Press, 2005)

Hey, Crumbling Balcony! Poems New & Selected (ECW Press, 2003)

Razovsky at Peace (ECW Press, 2001)

Farmer Gloomy's New Hybrid (ECW Press, 1999)

Henry Kafka & Other Stories (The Mercury Press, 1997)

The Inspiration Cha-Cha (ECW Press, 1996)

The Mud Game (w/ Gary Barwin, The Mercury Press, 1995)

The Pig Sleeps (w/ Mark Laba, Contra Mundo Books, 1993)

He Counted His Fingers, He Counted His Toes (Proper Tales Press, 1979)

The Thing in Exile (w/ Steve Feldman & Mark Laba,

Books by Kids, 1976)

the book of grief
and hamburgers

stuart
ross

Copyright © Stuart Ross, 2022

Published by ECW Press
665 Gerrard Street East
Toronto, Ontario, Canada M4M 1Y2
416-694-3348 / info@ecwpress.com

All rights reserved. No part of this publication may be reproduced, stored in a retrieval system, or transmitted in any form by any process — electronic, mechanical, photocopying, recording, or otherwise — without the prior written permission of the copyright owners and ECW Press. The scanning, uploading, and distribution of this book via the Internet or via any other means without the permission of the publisher is illegal and punishable by law. This book may not be used for text and data mining, AI training, and similar technologies. Please purchase only authorized electronic editions, and do not participate in or encourage electronic piracy of copyrighted materials. Your support of the author's rights is appreciated.

Editor for the Press: Michael Holmes
Copy-editor: Emily Schultz
Cover art: Angie Quick
Author photo: Stephen Brockwell

Library and Archives Canada Cataloguing in Publication

Title: The book of grief and hamburgers / Stuart Ross.

Names: Ross, Stuart, 1959- author.

Identifiers: Canadiana (print) 2021034427X | Canadiana (ebook) 20210344318

ISBN 978-1-77041-656-7 (softcover)
ISBN 978-1-77305-955-6 (ePub)
ISBN 978-1-77305-956-3 (PDF)
ISBN 978-1-77305-957-0 (Kindle)

Subjects: LCSH: Death. | LCSH: Bereavement. | LCSH: Grief. | LCGFT: Creative nonfiction.

Classification: LCC PS8585.O841 B66 2022 | DDC C814/.54—dc23

We acknowledge the support of the Canada Council for the Arts. *Nous remercions le Conseil des arts du Canada de son soutien.* This book is funded in part by the Government of Canada. *Ce livre est financé en partie par le gouvernement du Canada.* We acknowledge the support of the Ontario Arts Council (OAC), an agency of the Government of Ontario, which last year funded 1,965 individual artists and 1,152 organizations in 197 communities across Ontario for a total of $51.9 million. We also acknowledge the support of the Government of Ontario through the Ontario Book Publishing Tax Credit, and through Ontario Creates.

Printed and bound in Canada   Printing: Marquis   5 4 3 2

In memory of Michael Dennis

"We are the lucky men."

"I want to talk to my dad, but my dad is dead now. I know we can't have a regular conversation so I am trying to stay open to alternatives."

— Amy Fusselman, *The Pharmacist's Mate*

•

Somebody give me a hamburger.

          And he balanced a hamburger on his head.

She deals in rubber bands and hamburgers.

          For God's sake, look after our hamburgers.

      Who stole Grandpa's hamburger?

          Four score and seven
          hamburgers were how many.

        After he shaved his chin, he shaved his
        hamburger.

      Not with a bang, but a hamburger.

•

Hamburgers crept into my poetry in my late teens, about ten years after I started writing. They appeared a few years after I'd discovered David McFadden's poetry, and Stephen Crane's, and E. E. Cummings's, and Victor Coleman's, and Joe Rosenblatt's. I don't know if hamburgers appeared in any of those guys' poems. Well, maybe in David McFadden's, but if so, probably not for the same reason they appeared in my poems.

Sometimes the hamburgers in my poems were actual hamburgers. Sometimes they were Frank Sinatra. Sometimes the hamburgers that showed up in my poems were rubber bands. Once they were onion rings. Sometimes they were Frank Stella and Joe Hardy. Or penguins.

The lines on the previous page are not lines from my poems. But they could be. Most of them would likely be last lines. Does a hamburger make any line of poetry better? I mean, better than it was before it had a hamburger in it?

Other poets put an angel in their poems to make them better — sometimes the tongues of men and angels.

Or the moon. The moon is very popular among poets. Some people put love in their poem to make the poem a good poem.

When I worked with Dave McFadden on his volume of selected poems, *Why Are You So Sad?*, I thought we would reproduce the poems exactly as they had been originally published, and in chronological order. But first the order thing: Dave wanted them to appear in random order. He presented me with a random order for the poems in the book, but I think the order wasn't entirely random. Dave was wily that way. But the other thing: Dave wanted to edit his poems for this new volume. He was a better poet now than when he had originally written those poems in the 1960s and 1970s and 1980s, and he could make those poems better. In several of his poems from the 1960s, Dave replaced the word *love* with the word *thing*. And it was true: it made the poems better.

So Dave was a poet who put the word *love* into his poems when he was in his twenties and took the word *love* out of his poems when he was in his sixties.

Here's what I do: I put the word *hamburger* in my poems when things are getting a little too heavy. Because the word *hamburger* makes you laugh. So this manoeuvre makes a heavy poem lighter. You can lift it more easily.

•

My mother was an artist, which she mostly expressed
through being a self-taught interior decorator. She also
made some clay sculptures. Two of them are on a shelf
behind me right now, above the rows of old R & B and
Black gospel records I used to spin on my radio show.
One of the clay sculptures is of a ballerina, sitting cross-
legged. Or perhaps she is just a woman in tights. The
other sculpture my mother made and I kept is of our dog
Mousse. Mousse was a toy poodle whose pedigree name
was Parquet Ralphy of Russell Hill Road. We called him
Mousse. The sculpture has Mousse sitting, with one of his
paws raised slightly, as if he is hoping to shake your hand,
or as if you had just said, "Shake, Mousse. That's a good
boy. Shake." The sculpture, like Mousse, is mostly white
but with a black nose and black eyes, and some brown
flecks in his fur. It is covered in a glaze.

When I was six or seven years old, my mother took me to
the Art Gallery of Ontario to see a gigantic hamburger
made of painted fabric. It was taller than me. This
sculpture is called *Floor Burger*. It was created by Claes
Oldenburg in 1962. A burger nestled within a bun, and
a pickle perched on top. Some of the paint was already

beginning to crack and flake, even in 1966, when I first saw the gigantic hamburger.

A hamburger can be art. That is the first lesson about art I ever learned.

Claes Oldenburg was born ten days before my mother. He is still alive. My mother died in 1995. David McFadden died in 2018.

●

If I was the kind of writer who worked hard, I would look through all the books I've written, read over all my poems from the 1970s until the present, locate every mention of hamburgers, and tell you which of my poems have hamburgers in them. A lot of my poems have hamburgers.

But I do not work hard and my standards are low.

Also, my books are scattered everywhere throughout my home, and it would take me too long to find them.

•

Hamburgers are a device.

If my poems are getting too serious, I insert a hamburger. Hamburgers, like the word *hamburger*, make people laugh.

I haven't eaten a hamburger since 1993. That's when I became a vegetarian, but I forget why.

Oh yeah, I remember. I stopped eating meat and stopped adding salt to my food and stopped drinking coffee for reasons having to do with blood pressure. And then later my reason for not eating meat became that eating meat was not nice to animals.

I admit that when I go to an Indian buffet, I always take one piece of tandoori chicken. But what with this pandemic, I don't know if buffets will exist anymore.

Do you see what is happening?

I just realized what is happening.

I use hamburgers to deflect when my poems get too serious, or when they are about something so serious that

I become uncomfortable. A onetime friend of mine —
we were very close friends until he decided we weren't
— I'll call him K. (not Franz Kafka), was the one who
pointed that out to me. "You put hamburgers in your
poems whenever they're getting too serious. You deke the
seriousness by making readers laugh."

K. also said he was bothered by vegetarians who liked to
eat fake meat. "If you want to eat meat, then eat meat.
Don't eat tofu shaped like a hot dog."

Or like a hamburger!

I don't know why it was any skin off his back if
vegetarians ate tofu that looked like meat.

Oh, but look, I'm still doing it.

I am talking about hamburgers instead of talking about
grief.

When you call your dog Mousse, you must continually explain to people what kind of mousse you are talking about. You are talking about, you say, the French dessert, not the large-antlered vegetarian mammal.

You know what an elk is? Same thing. But our dog was the dessert.

But also not Big Moose from the Archie comics. Big Moose was big and dumb and a swell guy. He dated Midge and was friends with Jughead, who was asexual and whose only love was hamburgers. Most of what Jughead talked about was hamburgers. He was like Wimpy from *Popeye* but more relatable to kids. Maybe because he wore a crown-shaped beanie people called a "whoopee cap." Maybe just because he was in high school.

Did Jughead and Wimpy obsess over hamburgers to avoid their grief?

Did Jughead or Wimpy ever sit shiva? Did they ever sit shiva during a global pandemic?

Don't be stupid. They weren't Jewish. The hamburgers they ate were not kosher. A rabbi didn't bless the slaughterhouse where the meat in their hamburgers came from. With hamburgers made of tofu, the kind that annoyed K., you don't have to worry about whether they are kosher. You can even eat them with a glass of milk and it's still kosher.

Jughead and Wimpy, they probably ate their hamburgers with a big glass of milk.

•

Although Franz Kafka was not a moose, he was a vegetarian. Here's what the author of *Amerika* and *The Metamorphosis* and *The Trial* wrote to Grete Bloch:

> *And if the deterioration of the teeth wasn't actually due to inadequate care, then it was due, as with me, to eating meat. One sits at table laughing and talking (for me at least there is the justification that I neither laugh nor talk), and meanwhile tiny shreds of meat between the teeth produce germs of decay and fermentation no less than a dead rat squashed between two stones.*

Grete Bloch was a friend of Felice Bauer, Franz Kafka's fiancée. Kafka and Felice became engaged for the first time on the Jewish holiday Shavuot in 1914. Kafka wrote to Grete later that year, when he and Felice were having a hard time. Among other things he discussed in those letters was the health of his teeth.

Franz Kafka died of tuberculosis in 1924. Grete Bloch died in Auschwitz in 1944. Felice Bauer died in New York State in 1960.

•

Shavuot is about two things: it celebrates the wheat harvest in Israel and it marks the anniversary of when God gave Moses the Torah. I have been a Jew for sixty-one years but I didn't know that until now, when I just looked it up.

Shavuot falls each year sometime between mid-May and mid-June. My brother Barry died three months ago, on June 2. I haven't yet been able to grieve for him properly. Also, I don't know what it means to grieve properly. Unless you are a really religious Jew, you also don't know what the holiday Shavuot is all about.

Since I was a teenager, I have suffered from insomnia. Lately, temazepam, CBD oil, and indica chocolate have occasionally helped me sleep. I mean, I don't take all of them every night. I choose one and keep changing it up so my body doesn't know what to expect and so my body doesn't outsmart me.

If you are a really religious Jew, you stay up all night on Shavuot and study the Torah. When I stay up all night, I read the news, bug my cat, lie on my back, and worry. Sometimes my heart pounds and I wonder if I'm dying.

Because Shavuot is an agricultural thing, at least in part, it is a pretty big deal on the kibbutzes in Israel. My cousin Henia, who is really my mother's cousin, even though I call her my cousin, visited us in Toronto in maybe 1975. She has lived on a kibbutz in Israel all her life. Coming to Canada was a big deal. Henia didn't visit Canada again until 2018, which means she got to see Barry one more time before he died, but she never again got to see my other brother, Owen, or my parents, Syd and Shirley.

Somebody give me a hamburger.

•

The British poet, translator, and critic Michael Hamburger, who was born in Berlin but raised in London, translated, from the German, the works of Hölderlin, Grass, Enzensberger, Rilke, Celan, Sachs, Trakl, and Brecht.

He did not translate Franz Kafka.

Although he was a guy who translated the works of other writers, he also wrote his own poems, which I had never read until this past hour, when I looked them up. (This is called "research.") In his poem "Mad Lover, Dead Lady," he wrote:

> *She laughs when I tell her*
> *What it's like to be dead.*

Part of my grief, perhaps, is wanting my mother, my father, my brothers, and also Richard Huttel, John Lavery, Dave McFadden, Nelson Ball, and Lily — the dog in my adult life — to tell me what it's like to be dead.

Nelson chose the moment of his death. I sat in a chair at the foot of his hospital bed, and his friends Catherine and Suzan sat in chairs to his left. It was sad and it was peaceful. But Nelson was happy. Since he'd made this decision several days earlier, he was happy. In fact, he was eager.

I have always wondered if I should have asked him, in that fifteen-minute window he allowed us to be with him before the medical team entered the room, to tell me what his thoughts were on that last morning. The last morning he would ever wake up.

That morning, he was a person who knew with certainty when he woke up that it would be the last time he'd wake up.

Nelson was tall and thin, like so many of his poems. He ate little, and not well. I remember that he and his wife, the painter and writer Barbara Caruso, sometimes shared a can of Campbell's soup for lunch.

A few years after Barbara died, Nelson met Catherine. He often asked Catherine to bring him a hamburger from Harvey's when she came to visit.

Maybe I already told you, but I can't remember what a hamburger tastes like.

•

It may be that I have grieved and grieved, but I did not
recognize it because I don't know what grief is. I have
felt pain in my chest and at the same time an unfulfillable
longing. Tears have trickled down my cheeks. I am a man
of sixty-one and tears often trickle down my cheeks. I sob
and curse.

I don't know if this is anger or frustration or sadness.
I don't know if it is sadness, the degree of sadness that
reaches the depths that people identify as "grief."

Do you like pickles on your hamburger? Mayo? I've got
some grainy mustard in the fridge. Pull up a chair.

·

I became closer with Nelson Ball after the death of Barbara Caruso. They had been together for forty-four years. Nelson's grief was profound. He wrote many poems about Barbara after she died. Once when Catherine was upstairs in Barbara's studio, Nelson heard her footsteps through the floor from downstairs. It was like he was hearing Barbara's footsteps.

He wrote a poem about it.

When Nelson died, I took many things from his stationery storage closet as well as from his mailing room. From his mailing room, I took his long-armed stapler. From his stationery storage closet, I took a box of staples.

Perhaps the most famous book about grief in the English language is *A Grief Observed*, by C. S. Lewis. He wrote the book to document his bereavement after the death of his wife, Joy Davidman. In the book, he called her *H*. Lewis published *A Grief Observed* under the pseudonym N. W. Clerk. After he died, only three years after Joy's death, his own name appeared on subsequent editions of the book.

After my mother died, in 1995, when I was thirty-five, my friend Mary gave me a copy of *A Grief Observed*, by C. S. Lewis, hoping it might comfort me in my grief. "Ignore the God stuff," she suggested, knowing I was an atheist.

A funny thing is that several of C. S. Lewis's friends gave him a copy of *A Grief Observed*, by N. W. Clerk, hoping it might comfort him in his grief.

Nelson Ball was an atheist. C. S. Lewis was a Christian who became an atheist who became a Christian. Joy Davidman was an atheist who was a Jew who became a Christian. Barbara Caruso was an agnostic.

Joy Davidman was a poet. In "Prayer Before Daybreak," she wrote:

> *I have loved some ghost or other all my years.*
> *Dead men, their kisses and their fading eyes*
> *dim in the house of memory; glimmers*
> *in twilight air, no more.*

C. S. Lewis's first name was Clive. His second name was Staples.

•

In the thrift store I was looking at books. Being in a thrift store — when I don't walk in to seek anything in particular — is a way of avoiding things. It is a way, for example, of avoiding work. The thrift store is, in this way, my work's hamburger.

On the fiction shelf I found a book that was neither fiction nor poetry. It was about the Marx Brothers. It was filled with photos but seemed to be about a movie the Marx Brothers never made. I immediately recognized it as a rarity and wanted to buy the book for my brother Barry because if there was anything Barry loved, it was the Marx Brothers. He was always reading me clever Marx Brothers dialogue over the phone. He also liked Abbott and Costello, W. C. Fields, and the Three Stooges. When we were kids, we all watched the Three Stooges together on TV. Grown men poking each other in the eyes.

But I couldn't buy the book for my brother Barry because Barry is dead. Nyuk nyuk nyuk.

Today I was reading an essay by Lydia Davis. I don't remember the name of the essay, but it was about her influences as a writer. She talked about Robert Walser and also Franz Kafka because they both wrote some very short and strange stories that were a big influence on her. She talked about Russell Edson, who was also an influence on her and also an influence on me. Then she started talking about some poets.

Lydia Davis writes really short stories. Some of them are just one sentence long.

She thinks that maybe she is a poet. Or she doesn't care whether people call what she writes fiction or poetry. Or she doesn't think there is a difference between fiction and poetry. I can't remember.

If I was a writer who researched diligently, I would go and read that essay again and find out.

But when she started talking about poets, she quoted a very small poem by Lorine Niedecker. I immediately wanted to write to Nelson Ball and tell him. Lorine Niedecker was his favourite poet. But I can't tell him that Lydia Davis quoted Lorine Niedecker in her essay because Nelson is dead. He died on August 16, 2019. I was with his friends Catherine and Suzan. Catherine held his hand as his breathing stopped.

Grace held Barry's hand after his breathing had stopped and she found him.

It's really funny. I almost wrote "after his grieving had stopped" in that last sentence. When I say "almost," I mean I thought it for half a second. Another half second I spent thinking about something was when I thought I would buy that book about the Marx Brothers for Barry, and another half second was the one I spent thinking about telling Nelson about Lydia Davis quoting a poem by Lorine Niedecker.

The next half second I spent wondering if Nelson had ever read Lydia Davis. Then I spent a half second wondering if Nelson had ever heard of Lydia Davis.

Nelson had about two hundred thousand books in his home on Willow Street in Paris, Ontario, which was also his bookstore. Not one of those books was by Lydia Davis.

•

Before I opened my eyes, I saw a black police car rolling slowly past me. Barry was in the back. He hadn't paid his debts. I blew him a kiss but I could see he was angry and yelling.

Then I opened my eyes. It was a relief to be awake. Had I been grieving while I slept?

For years after my mother died, I dreamed of things like:

- she's making us all dinner at the condo on Finch Avenue, and we are sad because she doesn't realize she is dead;
- she's telling us about her day, but we're just thinking, "Oh, you don't know you're not alive and so you just keep on doing what you did when you were alive."

When I open my eyes, it is a relief to be awake. I pull myself out of bed and brush my teeth. I am living in a world, at a time, when I will never talk with my mother again. I will never talk with my father again. Or Owen. Or Barry.

Sometimes it makes me want to make it so I am also not alive.

•

Hamburger to the right of them, hamburger to the left of them.

How much is that hamburger in the window? Woof woof.

When is a hamburger not a hamburger? When it turns into a . . .

I took the hamburger for a walk in the blizzard.

I fear for our hamburgers, I fear for their souls.

Mr. Hamburger, I presume?

Inside of a hamburger, it's too dark to read.

•

In the last several years, I have lost several close writer friends, some of whom were also mentors.

I lost the Acadian fiction writer and songwriter John Lavery, who lived in Gatineau and spoke in such a low tone, his voice such a deep rumble, that you had to lean in to hear him, just as perhaps he leaned in to hear me when I MC'd his celebration of life with his daughter Madeleine.

I lost the film theorist and professor Robin Wood, who lived a few blocks from me when I lived with Lillian in downtown Toronto. Robin changed the way I watched films and read books. He changed the way I thought and also introduced me to rogan josh and Fauré's *Requiem*.

I lost the essayist and painter Barbara Caruso, who lived in Paris, Ontario, with her husband, Nelson Ball, and who, with severe arthritis, painted and drew nearly 1,500 works of precise abstract art and kept a constant journal. When I visited, she sometimes had a list of written questions she'd ask me.

I lost the Chicago poet and playwright Richard Huttel, who lived his last years at his sister Diane's home in Albuquerque and flew to Toronto one last time when Laurie and I got married; I recorded him reading his poems on the beach at Lake Ontario. The wind blowing off the water obscured his voice.

I lost Dave McFadden, writer of poetry, fiction, and travelogues, and one of the three or four greatest influences on my work. He was born in Hamilton, died in Toronto, and I was lucky to have edited his final six books. Steve Venright and I delivered his eulogy as his ashes sat in the front of the church in a Dilbert cookie jar.

I lost the poet and bookseller Nelson Ball, the husband of the painter and essayist Barbara Caruso, who found a sustaining platonic love in the last years of his life, and whose final five books of poetry I edited, and whose literary executor I became, and twelve of whose bookcases — he built hundreds of them — I took from his home on Willow Street in Paris, Ontario.

I have grieved all these people — if what I do when I remember the dead is grieving. And there are other close friends I know I will soon be grieving. It's probably bad luck to name them. It's probably bad luck to name those who may soon be dead.

My friend Michael Dennis, who is like a brother to me, tells me he has only months to live. Usually a loquacious conversationalist, he doesn't find much to talk about with me these days, but we talk often. I am reading his poems. I am finding old correspondence from him, actual letters he sent in the mail, some from as far back as the early 1980s.

Look, here is a book of his he sent me. He has handwritten a poem on the padded envelope. It is dated June 16, 2005. He probably didn't keep a copy of it for himself.

THE VANIER GRILL
poem for Stuart Ross

you're thinking you'll flip a coin
heads it's to the strippers
and seeing what's up there
tails and it's Beethoven, the 9th
and all that comes with that.

later, at a diner
some of the ladies straggle in
they've exhausted themselves
with either dancing or the cello

they order black coffee
we finish our burgers
head home
talking poetry

I don't want Michael to be gone. I want to talk poetry with him forever. Though I am a vegetarian, I want to eat burgers with him.

Burgers, burgers, everywhere burgers.

I sat with Nelson Ball in his kitchen, which was also his living room. He had emphysema and was hooked up to an oxygen tank. Some people need supplemental oxygen because they are climbing Mount Everest. Nelson couldn't even climb to the second floor of his house, where his late wife Barbara's studio still stood just as she left it, as if she were working on a new canvas.

I don't think Nelson would have liked me using the adjective "late." He once told me how much he disliked the euphemism "passed away." This is when we were discussing my being his literary executor. I must have said, "After you've passed away . . ."

"I don't like that phrase. It's *dead*. After I'm dead . . ."

"No, I don't like it either. I don't know why I said it. How about 'croaked'?"

"That's another euphemism. It's 'dead.'"

"I think 'croak' is even stronger than 'dead.'"

When I asked him if he would like there to be a volume of his collected poems after his death, he replied, "I don't care. I'll be dead."

When I asked him if he would like there to be a volume of his letters to other writers after his death, he replied, "I'll be dead."

When I asked him if he would like there to be a volume of his poems for Barbara after his death, he replied, "I'll be dead."

A couple of days before his medically assisted death, for which he was eager and even impatient, Suzan asked him again, on my behalf, if he'd like there to be a book of his collected poems after he's gone. He smiled very slightly and nodded.

But he did know that he wanted a biography written of Barbara, and he asked Lola Lemire Tostevin, a poet and biographer and essayist, to write it. She is writing it.

So, that book Mary gave me, *A Grief Observed*, by C. S.
Lewis. I read it when my mother died after some
unfortunate turns a cancer surgery took. I ignored the
God stuff.

My mother's death at sixty-six was devastating: we were
very close and I, like the rest of my family, had been in
constant denial about the seriousness of her illness.
She wasn't actually going to die. There was no way
she'd die.

The book offered some comfort. At least by being a
distraction from grief while I read it.

After my brother Barry's death a few months ago,
a death during a pandemic, I poked around my
disorganized bookshelves for that book by Clive Staples
Lewis. Or maybe it was in one of the fifty boxes of
books in my basement I hadn't unpacked since I'd
moved to Cobourg a decade earlier. The hours it would
take to dig it up weren't worth it, and I saw that I
could buy an eBook version for $2.50. I bought it. This
morning I began reading it. It is a smart book, from
its very first sentence, a sentence I had forgotten but

that my therapist, Stephen Ticktin, remembered in a conversation last week:

No one ever told me that grief felt so like fear.

I can't completely wrap my brain around that. But I feel that the fear I might have felt with my mother's death when I was thirty-five is very different from the fear I felt with my brother Owen's when I was forty or my dad's when I was still forty, but especially different from how I experienced the death of my brother Barry when I was sixty and already far more preoccupied with my own mortality.

No one ever told me that hamburgers felt so much like fear.

No one ever told me that fear felt so much like hamburgers.

No one ever told a hamburger that grief felt so like fear.

Or that fear felt so like hamburgers.

To search for a single word in a physical book is time-consuming. If you recall the particular word, you may remember that it appeared, for example, in the top third of a left-hand page somewhere in the first half of the book. But with electronic books, you can just do a search.

The word *hamburger* does not appear in *A Grief Observed*.

The word *burger* does not appear in *A Grief Observed*.

C. S. Lewis does not veer from his subject matter; he does not hide or evade. There are no hamburgers, culinary or metaphorical, in his book *A Grief Observed*.

As I write these words, I wonder when I will turn unflinchingly to my own grief in this book. That is the particular corner I am trying to paint myself into. But I worry that I may be too clever for myself. Or too weak.

Too frightened? Too flinchful?

•

I am the only person in my family who will have died in the correct order.

My father, who should have died first, died third.

My mother, who should have died second, died first.

My brother Barry, who should have died third, died fourth.

My brother Owen, who should have died fourth, died second.

I should die fifth and I will. Look how orderly I am.

I worry what I might have done had I been a Jew in Poland in 1942.

•

It is two days into 2021 and so much in the world has changed. I am reading through the manuscript for this book, which I mostly finished in the third week of December.

I just read that line I wrote on the previous page:

> *I worry what I might have done had I been a Jew in Poland in 1942.*

I have no idea what I meant by that.

I search its context and still I have no idea.

I worry that it may be an early sign of dementia that I wrote that.

But I am convinced it is important. Perhaps I am now less smart than I was two weeks ago. I am going to trust the brain that wrote it two weeks ago.

•

In stuff there is grief.

It's possible someone said that.

Is it grief if it is over stuff?

Someone else might have said that.

I sat in my father's walk-in closet and went through
his clothes. I chose some shirts for myself. A few pairs
of socks. I took his tefillin, which were almost for sure
his father's tefillin — Max Razovsky's — and maybe
someone else dead's tefillin before that. I took a set of
his cufflinks. And a ring that is not a wedding ring, but
perhaps a ring from the Independent Order of Odd
Fellows or from his bowling league.

I took my father's bowling-ball bag. I don't think I
took the bowling ball. He used to win turkeys with his
bowling. As a family, we did not like turkey. We also did
not celebrate Thanksgiving. I thought Thanksgiving was
a gentile holiday, like Easter and Christmas and Simcoe
Day. I still don't know for sure.

Everything in my father's walk-in closet was something my father had touched. My father had been in this walk-in closet every day. When my father died, I looked out the window of his twenty-second-floor condominium, facing north from near Toronto's north boundary, and I realized that God was dead.

I'm an atheist, but still it was shocking that God was dead. Who would I measure my actions against? Had I ever measured my actions against my father's actions?

I cried on the phone when I told my father's friends that he had died. I sobbed and gasped to find my words.

Chubby Allen said, "Get ahold of yourself, Stuart."

Everything in Barry's small office smelled like smoke. Every sheet of paper. Every photograph. Every baseball trophy. They smelled like cigarettes.

I sobbed and I cursed Barry.

Is anger grief?

"Grief" is a postcard published in 1985 by jwcurry, a friend I met in the late 1970s while I was selling my chapbooks on the streets in downtown Toronto. It is a silkscreened reproduction of an "ad" I drew. I say it is an ad because in the bottom left-hand corner, it says, PURCHASE GLIT DIAMONDS. That always makes john and me laugh.

But the expression of grief itself. A man stands on a skyscraper at night and howls into the empty sky. I think it's a pretty good depiction of grief.

I hadn't experienced much grief in 1985. I'd lost a grandfather, Samuel Blatt; an uncle, Sol Mainster; and a dog, Rufus. But the futility of the howl I drew when I was twenty-six is how I feel now when I am almost sixty-two.

It is like screaming into a pillow.

It is like yelling to bring someone back to life.

It is like trying to make everyone hear me and understand me.

Futility.

Does one ever recover from grief?

But also: does my postcard depict a commodification
of grief? Can grief be used to sell diamonds? Or
hamburgers?

When I drew that picture, did I think it was funny or did
I think it was sad?

I think I thought it was both.

The picture, I mean. Not grief.

•

Sometimes I feel like I've definitely had my share of grief.
I can't really handle any more because I haven't caught
up with the bereavement already on my plate.

It's like working on an assembly line and I haven't done
the thing with the gizmo I'm holding that I'm supposed
to do and more and more gizmos are piling up.

Tonight I received a message from my friend Michael in
Ottawa. He is "struggling."

It is hard to imagine a world without Michael Dennis.
But I know there'll be a world after he's gone, just as
there was still a world after my mother's death and my
father's and Dave McFadden's and Richard Huttel's.

It'll just be a different world. A world that's not as good.

But the thought of saying goodbye to Michael is
unbearable. Michael had a wooden plaque made for
the door to the guest room in the house where he lives
with Kirsty, whom he calls K. in his poems. I have
stayed in that guest room scores of times over the last
couple of decades. It is packed with books and art, like

the rest of their home. The plaque says, *The Stuart Ross Reading Room.*

We had a stupid fight around the time that plaque was installed. How I regret that fight. Our growing back together took some months, some bumpy months. How I regret the lost time that stupid fight caused. My stubbornness caused. Maybe his too. How I regret that I caused his mind and his body to feel anger. That's not something you want to cause in someone you love.

My brother Barry and I also had a fight. It was about politics. We had very different political views. Mine veer to the left, like our parents'. Barry's veered somewhere I just didn't understand. Our fight meant we didn't speak for a full year.

But I knew I had to renew contact with him. We were the last two brothers left. Owen was dead. Barry and I had to talk. Our parents would be horrified to know we weren't talking.

So we talked again. We agreed not to discuss politics anymore. We had another year to not talk politics before he died.

I hope Michael is comfortable now. I hope he is resting. It's possible he can't get up the stairs to sleep anymore. It's possible he now goes downstairs to sleep. In the Stuart Ross Reading Room.

Michael, I worry that I am too tired from grieving to grieve for you too.

But at the same time, I don't even know if I have grieved. I still can't figure out exactly what grieving is. Maybe because it's a thing that doesn't seem to ever end. If I grieved right, wouldn't it end? If it's a constant state, isn't it just living?

Whenever I drive from Cobourg to Ottawa along Highway 7, I pass a big burger shack on the north side of the road. When I get to Ottawa, Michael tells me they serve the best hamburger he's ever tasted.

Please let Michael have another hamburger.

•

I have this terrible feeling that the last time Owen and I spoke involved me yelling at him. I am leaving it in the category of "feeling" because I think it is a fact, and I don't want to admit it.

Once when we were kids, Owen went and had a talk with a bully who had bullied me. That guy never bullied me again.

Also, Owen loved watching professional wrestling on TV. So did my grandfather, Samuel Blatt. Owen taught me how to do a full nelson on somebody. He liked hockey, and horse races, and Chicago 58 salami. I liked books, and music, and giant fabric hamburgers.

I can't remember now if Owen was forty-four or forty-six when he fell to the floor and called for our father. And I can no longer call Barry to ask because he also fell to the floor. Whatever age Owen was, I am way more years than that now and yet he is still my older brother.

•

I was text-chatting on Skype with my friend Dag T. Straumsvåg. Dag, a poet and translator who lives in Trondheim, Norway, has become close to Michael through email; he is a big fan of Michael's poetry and translated a selection of Michael's poems — as he has a selection of mine and of Nelson Ball's.

After Michael's cancer diagnosis, Dag worked hard to finish those translations, and he published them as a beautiful chapbook through his new imprint, A + D, a publishing project he and his girlfriend, Angella, started this year. She lives in Minnesota; they've never met in person.

Along with a friend of Michael's, Bruce McEwen, I helped with printing and logistics. It was a team effort so that Michael would be able to hold that book in his hands. The book is called *Spøkjelse i japanske drosjar* — *Ghosts in Japanese Taxis.* Michael sure did hold it in his hands: his poems in Nynorsk.

I asked Dag if any of his own poems mentioned hamburgers. I'm looking for as many hamburgers as I can find.

A few minutes later, Dag sent me a poem of his, one of what he calls his "haiku strings." The poem is called "A Hamburger in the Night." It is dedicated to Angella. It's an intense, lively poem that goes all over the place. It goes all over the place, and then it ends:

> *Rushing by outside   we're going for hamburgers*
> *& coffee you say   I take a deep drag   of another*
> *cigarette   in this small building   Not meant for*
> *driving   trying to make up my mind   if I want*
> *French fries   With my hamburger*

It sounds a bit like a Charles Bukowski poem. Our friend Michael likes Bukowski's poems and also his novels — he has every book of Bukowski's ever published, and he has a letter Bukowski wrote him back when he once wrote to Bukowski. I think it's framed.

Dag and I talk a lot about Michael these days. I know that Dag feels a bit helpless, being so far away.

I am a little over three hours away from Michael and Kirsty, but in the pandemic era, it's a nearly insurmountable distance. Since the pandemic was declared, I have driven to Ottawa three times to visit.

Michael, who once held court in any social situation, has very few words to offer now, at least when he and I are talking.

Dag says Michael's emails are getting shorter and shorter.

This morning I sent to the printer a book of collaborative poems Michael and I wrote at his kitchen table over the course of three years, during six marathon writing sessions. By marathon, I mean three hours and fifteen minutes. Every single time we met to collaborate, it took us three hours and fifteen minutes to write twenty poems.

The book will be ready in five to seven business days.

The book is called *70 Kippers: The Dagmar Poems*.

I fear that it won't be long before every time I hold that book I will feel sad. Am I already grieving?

But I want to think that every time I hold that book I will feel comforted by the memory of a friendship I am so lucky to have.

Earlier in Dag's poem, he writes:

> *Cleaning the brass plaques   of the stumbling*
> *stones laid down   in front of my house   Lily*
> *Dvoretsky   her mother & her brother   Marie &*
> *Sigurd   Murdered in Auschwitz   they lived here*
> *where I live now*

Dag has written a poem that contains both the Holocaust and a hamburger.

•

The phone rings. It's Richard Huttel. He has called to tell me he has late-stage brain cancer.

> *(I'm writing in the present tense, but this is something that happened in 2013 or 2014. I am using the present tense because I want Richard to still be alive.)*

I love the big guy from Chicago who is Richard Huttel. He tells me a few years later, with maybe a hint of pride, that he has the same brain cancer that U.S. war hero and Republican senator John McCain has just been diagnosed with. He sends me links to articles about it. I don't read them.

Richard is what is called a "swing voter." He has voted both Republican and Democrat. Plus, he's a poet who works in a bank, just like Canadian poet Raymond Souster was. John McCain is a "maverick" politician who outrages members of both parties. But they all admire him, maybe partly because he pisses them off. This might be why Richard is proud to have the same brain cancer that John McCain has.

I met Richard around the same time I met Michael. It was 1980, and Richard was in Toronto with his new wife, Jayne, and they were walking along Yonge Street, and there I was, selling my poetry chapbooks. Maybe that day I was wearing the sign around my neck that said, "Writer Going to Hell: Buy My Books." Richard stopped and talked with me for a long time. He bought my book. Maybe it was *When Electrical Sockets Walked Like Men*. He was a poet too, he said. He was on his honeymoon. That was the start of a great friendship.

Some weeks later, I received a wonderful typewritten letter from him, stuffed with a few poems and a newsletter he published. That was the start of a great correspondence.

I didn't see Richard again in person until several years later. Jayne had died. Richard was grieving. They had a four-year-old son named Andy.

I told Richard to come to Toronto. I'd organize a reading for him in the living room of the Isabella Street apartment I shared with Lillian, sell advance tickets, and it would pay for the flights for him and Andy.

It worked. They came to Toronto. Andy never stopped talking for five days. The reading was superb. Somewhere, I have a cassette tape of it. A great American poet had read in my living room!

Richard came back to Toronto every year or two after that. I wished he would move here.

The last time he came, in the second or third year of his cancer, he came to carry Laurie's ring to me during our wedding ceremony. At the wedding, I also handed him copies of a book of his selected poems I'd published called *That Said*. He'd never had a full-length collection and I wanted to be sure he got to have one while he was alive.

Michael Dennis was in that room where the wedding happened; he held one corner of the chuppah. David McFadden was in that room. He read us some love haiku. Barry was in that room. He was one of the MCs, along with Laurie's brother Kevin.

The next year, I would visit Richard in Albuquerque, where he moved to live with Diane and Tim, his sister and brother-in-law. We sat on the back patio and played chess and listened to Rickie Lee Jones while peacocks wandered around our feet.

I would attend the celebration of life for him the year after that, in Chicago. It felt so strange to go to Flash Taco without him. To go to all those bookstores without him. To be in Wicker Park without him.

I sat on a bench in one of his favourite spots in Chicago and wrote a poem called "Chicago" for him. I wrote it in a style as if I were Nelson Ball writing.

When this pandemic ends, I want to go back to Chicago and go to Flash Taco with Richard.

A couple of months before he died, Richard phoned me and left a message. I didn't call him back. I don't know what was in my brain that let me not call him back. Perhaps cowardice. I will always regret that I didn't call him back.

●

CHICAGO

the foamy water
reaches
now
to the cold
blue sky

Richard
sat here too
on this wood bench
saw this too

now he is ash
in the grass
and in tree bark

in my hair
I hope

•

Seeing so many people around me die has occasionally made the idea of suicide seem like maybe something I should entertain.

Now that I live two blocks from Lake Ontario, I picture myself walking into the lake. I walk down the street and then I walk into the lake. I can't swim properly so this will be really effective.

It's a bad idea, though, for me, right now.

Not the worst idea, but a pretty bad one.

•

A movie that no one ever talks about is called *A Thousand Clowns*. It was made in 1965, directed by Fred Coe, written by Herb Gardner. I love that movie, and Mark Laba loves that movie.

Mark Laba's brother Michael was the first person I knew who died from HIV-related causes. At the time, in the early 1980s, I didn't know what it would feel like to have a brother who had died. I don't think I expressed enough sympathy to Mark, or expressed it in the right way.

It just occurred to me what a funny name "Herb Gardner" is.

One line in *A Thousand Clowns* that killed me and Mark was when the guy who Jason Robards plays goes into a restaurant. It's dark and atmospheric. The waiter comes up and asks if he can get Murray Burns, who is Jason Robards, anything.

"Yes. A hamburger and a flashlight."

•

This book feels like one big hamburger. My intention was to make myself face things I don't think I've succeeded in facing.

To frighten myself.

To make myself cry.

To make myself mourn.

To hurl myself into the bubbling vat of grief.

But I won't do it.

It's not like I don't cry, though. I cry pretty much every day, even if just for a moment.

But isn't grieving more than crying? Isn't it a "coming to terms"?

I have never come to terms.

I want to force myself to come to terms. That's what I'm trying to do here.

Won't you please join me?

•

I am a person who has had a lot of mentors. I'm lucky that way.

Here are my mentors who have died.

Robin Wood, the British-born gay/feminist/Freudian/ Marxist film theorist. Robin was the biggest influence on my life aside from my mother. A few weeks before he died in 2009, he dictated a list of his ten top films. They are *Rio Bravo*, *I Can't Sleep* or *I Don't Want to Sleep Alone*, *Sanshô Dayû*, *Tokyo Story*, *Ruggles of Red Gap* or *Make Way for Tomorrow*, *Code Inconnu*, *The Reckless Moment* or *Letter from an Unknown Woman*, *Angel Face*, *The Seven Samurai*, and *Le crime de Monsieur Lange* or *Le règle du jeu*. He snuck in a few extras with those ors.

Larry Fagin, the New York poet and writing teacher. I had maybe half a dozen sessions with Larry, in person and over the phone. He took me to Veselka, where he went every day for breakfast, and I got a twelve-dollar potato latke. Ron Padgett went to see him a few days before he died. He said Larry was in good spirits and lucid. I asked Ron to tell Larry what a big influence he was on me. I suspect they had other things to discuss.

David McFadden, the Hamilton and later Toronto poet. I fell in love with his poetry when I was a teenager and stumbled upon one of his collections at a library in North York. He showed me that you could write poetry like it was just a conversation a couple of people were having and you could write about serious things with humour. He didn't mention hamburgers in that context. In my twenties, I met him. We eventually became good friends. I loved his poetry and then I loved him.

John Lavery, the Gatineau fiction writer and musician. I once told you that John spoke in a low rumble; his voice blended into the background noise. Everything he said was important so it was worth the strain. I sent him some of my new short stories during the last year of his life. He wrote me back that we'd better discuss them soon, or we'd never get to. He was a brilliant thinker, an exquisite writer, an eccentric songwriter. We never discussed my short stories. I can still hear his voice.

bpNichol, the B.C.-born Toronto poet, fictioneer, songwriter, and visual artist. Wasn't he everyone's mentor? He snorted when he laughed: not a snort of derision but one of enthusiasm. I interviewed him in 1982 for my literary zine *Mondo Hunkamoga: A Journal of Small Press Stuff*. I was at his home on Admiral Street, in his study. I had a fever. I was delirious. He was so kind to me, he was always kind. I think he made me a mug of tea. He wore velour clothes. He died at forty-four, in 1988. He will always be an elder poet to me.

Nelson Ball, the Paris, Ontario, poet, How did we become so close? I edited his last five books and I'm editing yet another two now that he is gone. Before his home sold, the four-storey office building he lived in for nearly forty years — most of those with his wife, the uncompromising painter and writer Barbara Caruso — I rented a van and took a dozen of his bookcases. There were probably two hundred bookcases on Willow Street: he built them all by hand. Since Nelson's death, the home I share with Laurie has filled with the things of Nelson and Barbara.

Crad Kilodney, who I find it hard to talk about. The American-born Toronto writer and I were estranged for a decade before he died. He was an atheist who became religious when he was dying. I bet that happens a lot. I met Crad when he was selling his self-published fiction chapbooks on Yonge Street in the late 1970s. I joined him with my own self-published chapbooks. I learned so much from him, and at times I idolized him. He was a misanthrope. We played chess on weekends. He was a racist. Eventually I distanced myself from him. After his death, I read at a celebration of his life. I still felt ambivalent about him, but he had written some very fine passages.

Joe Rosenblatt, the poet and artist who once lived on Greensides in Toronto. But he died in Qualicum Beach, British Columbia. He taught at my high school, AISP, for a week when I was in Grade 13. Mark Laba was in that class too. Joe once folded a bad poem by one of the students into an airplane and flew it across the room. He once got Mark to photocopy copies of Mark's poems for the whole class, because Mark was the only actual poet among us. Joe liked the fried liver and onions in the school cafeteria. He went through scores of pages of my poems, saying, "Nothing worth salvaging here. Nothing worth salvaging here." Just one poem survived. He crossed half of it out and told me to work on it. It's called "Ritual of the Concrete Penguins."

I spoke on the phone yesterday to Steven. He was a friend of mine in childhood, and he is still a friend of mine, more than fifty years later. Our parents were very close friends. His parents are still alive, and they are in their early nineties.

I told Steven I was writing a book called *The Book of Grief and Hamburgers*. He said, "Why make a joke about it?"

I told him that was a very good question, and that it was the point of the book: in my writing, I have the habit of throwing in hamburgers when things get emotionally difficult.

He told me to go get his book of poetry, *In the Shallow Noise*. I hadn't read that book in many years. I went and got it. Luckily, I recently alphabetized my poetry books, so I could find it quickly, under Steven Alan Feldman.

He told me to look in his book for a poem called "Informal hamburger." I found it. This is how it reads:

Informal hamburger

I'm not saying I know everything about poems or everything about hamburgers, but that is a damn good poem about hamburgers.

I wish I had written it.

Steven's son is named Seth. That's what my parents were going to name me, except my grandmother, Nina Blatt, couldn't pronounce *th*.

Nina Blatt died when I was six months old.

Steven and I speak on the phone almost every week. When we say goodbye, we say, "I love you."

•

Is the death of one person the thing that launches grief?
What about two people? Or three or four? What happens
when your entire family is gone?

So many members of my family disappeared in the
Holocaust. How can I even complain about anything?

Am I mistaking self-pity for grief?

Yesterday, we learned that Richard Vaughan's body has been found by the Fredericton police. Richard went missing on the evening of Thanksgiving. My first fear on hearing that he'd gone missing was that he'd been murdered by gay-bashers. My second fear was that Richard had killed himself. Suicide is not always the best choice, but it is a choice.

Perhaps we all feared that Richard — who wrote poetry, plays, and essays, and made and performed art under the name R. M. Vaughan — would never be found and we would never know what happened to him.

The American poet Weldon Kees disappeared in 1955, on the day that would four years later be my birthday, July 18. His empty car was discovered the next day near the Golden Gate Bridge.

Many years after I was in high school, one of the teachers at the school disappeared. Her car was discovered near the Niagara River. She wrote children's books.

So far as I know, Richard Vaughan didn't have a car. I don't know if he even had a driver's licence.

He and I launched our first poetry books together in 1996. He had the idea that we would each begin by reading a poem by the other. It was a beautiful idea. We read aloud poems we had never read before, to the audience gathered for the ECW Press poetry launch. Then we launched our respective second books of poetry together in 1999. I remember less about that launch.

Richard and I were friends, but never close friends. But his death hits me in a visceral way. Perhaps because I related so much to him. Perhaps because I have thought about walking into the lake.

Yesterday I wrote to my therapist, who is an existentialist, and asked for a non-scheduled meeting. I want to talk with him about antidepressants. I took Wellbutrin for about a year in 2006. I didn't like it, though I think it helped. It made me feel like I was a mechanical device.

Everything tasted like tin.

I think I'd like to take it again, even though I don't want to take it again.

Richard was fifty-five years old. Six years younger than me. We both worked in the literary world. We once worked together at *eye Weekly* in Toronto. We both suffered from insomnia. In fact, one time I stayed up all night in a small hotel room in Montreal above a sex shop copy-editing a book-length essay he wrote about insomnia.

I find that maybe I am grieving Richard's death more fully than I have been able to grieve my brother's death four months earlier. My relationship with Richard was much less complicated. And, like I say, I identified with Richard.

I don't know how he died.

I don't know what his last thoughts were.

I don't know if he knew his last thoughts would be his last thoughts.

•

I am the only person left alive if you look at all the people who lived at 179 Pannahill Road when I grew up. Now they are all dead, except for me.

I grew up in the 1960s and the 1970s.

My first job was as a library page at Bathurst Heights Public Library. I took a bus to get there. I was paid $1.45 an hour when I started. On Saturdays I worked for seven hours. I earned $10.15. On the two weeknights I worked, I worked for two and a half hours. I earned $3.62 or $3.63. I'm not sure who got the extra half penny.

On Saturdays, I went for lunch at the greasy spoon diner in Lawrence Plaza. I ate a banquet burger. A banquet burger contains a burger, bacon, and a slice of orange cheese. For condiments, I chose ketchup.

The burger came wrapped in waxed paper and put into a brown paper bag.

It was not a fibre art sculpture.

I am avoiding things again.

•

Does Richard Vaughan have hamburgers in his poems?

I find my copy of his first poetry book, *A Selection of Dazzling Scarves*. I haven't read it for over two decades. I scan every page for a hamburger.

I find a pancake. I find Cheerios. I find cake. I find George Cukor, who is not food but a film director whom Robin Wood admired. I find sandwiches. I find cheese and I find bananas.

I have come to report that *A Selection of Dazzling Scarves* contains no hamburgers.

That should have been obvious to me. Richard Vaughan avoided nothing. Well, maybe he avoided things in his poems, but his poems sure are honest.

He was not a coward like I am.

Some people might say that if he had been more of a coward, he might still be alive.

Some people might say that if he had been less of a coward, he might still be alive.

His first book of poetry contains no hamburgers. He was not a coward like I am.

·

It's stupid to search my poetry books for hamburgers.

Though I bet there is a hamburger in one of Ron Padgett's poems. How could there not be?

And Tom Clark has a "vomburger" in one of his poems in *At Malibu*. I have loved Tom Clark's poetry since I was a teenager. I mentioned that to my poet friend Hoa Nguyen. She gave me his email address and told me I should tell him. I got up my nerve and did it. He wrote me back a short note and thanked me. He once posted my New Year's poem on his blog. In August 2018, he was hit by a car. He died the next day.

The only two men who kissed me when we said goodbye after a visit were Robin Wood and Michael Dennis. I kissed them back. In Robin's case, through his beard. They both drank a bottle of red wine with every dinner.

•

I haven't had a vivid dream in so long. But last night, a bad night for sleeping, I did get some sleep and had a dream.

In my dream, Laurie had stumbled upon a black-and-white photo I had never seen before. A group of people were sitting in a restaurant that had exposed-brick walls. It looked a little like Chez Piggy in Kingston. Chez Piggy was founded by Zal Yanovsky, who also founded the pop group the Lovin' Spoonful. My Hebrew name is Zalman, which maybe was Zal's full name.

In the photo, six people were lined up along one side of a table, the way people sit in movies or TV shows, so that the camera can see everyone from the front. From right to left were my father, my mother, Barry, Owen, my cousin Beverly, and my cousin Carla. My mother had a beautiful smile. Everyone looked like they were having a good time.

I was struck, in the dream, by the fact that I wasn't in the photo. But looking again, I saw that Owen looked to be about five years old, so I guess I wasn't born yet.

In the dream, I began to sob. I sobbed and sobbed, and Laurie showed me two more photos from the same scene. Each was only slightly different from the others. My dream-sobbing woke me up.

Was I sleep-grieving again?

When I think about my family — how all of them: my father, mother, Barry, and Owen, are dead — I feel adrift.

Is the sensation of being adrift grieving?

Why do I feel like I don't know how to grieve?

Do I think grieving is a way of getting past the sadness?

There is no getting past sadness.

•

I distract myself with news, with American politics. At this moment, we are in the worst wave of a worldwide viral pandemic, and at the same time, U.S. democracy is crumbling. I spend more time reading news online than I do meditating on the dead in my family.

And I am the last living member of my family, so the time I have left to live is the time my memories of Syd, Shirley, Owen, and Barry have left to live. Why am I wasting my time on the dissolution of the U.S.?

Laurie and I drove to Paris, Ontario, two weekends ago for what would be our last visit to Nelson Ball's home on Willow Street. We took home with us twelve bookcases, Barbara Caruso's swivel chair, the library cart that stood beside Nelson's chair in his living room, a floor lamp Nelson read by at his chair, a small table, scores of pieces of Barbara's art both for our home and to distribute to friends, and some books, cassettes, and CDs. Laurie also took some of Barbara's canvas and wooden frames to make her own art.

After ten years of living in Cobourg, I am finally able to unpack the fifty boxes of books that have been stored in the basement here on Division Street. We are turning that storeroom into a library and reading room, with the help of Nelson's shelves.

I am unpacking books I haven't seen in many years. Look, here's one now: *Why Do People Hate America?*, by Ziauddin Sardar and Merryl Wyn Davies, from 2002. A quick flip through this book I hadn't gotten around to reading, and here is chapter 4: "American Hamburgers and Other Viruses."

> *The hamburger is a particular source of hatred of America. It is the single most concentrated, or should that be congealed, symbol of the entire complex that is America. Like the hamburger, the idea of America has a number of separate ingredients. . . . Like the hamburger, this multi-dimensional America is reduced and experienced as a standardised, mass-produced, packaged brand. . . . It is the degree to which America proclaims and glories in itself as a compound whole that makes the hamburger such a powerful metaphor for the nation, and such a potent symbol and focus for criticism of America in the rest of the world. The hamburger is more than its ingredients — it is, indeed, a way of life.*

Or maybe a hamburger is just a hamburger. Can anything be only what it is?

The philosopher J. Krishnamurti suggested that we stare at a rock until we can see only the rock, and nothing beyond it, physically or metaphorically or historically. We must see the rock without interference by our ideas of rocks, our memories of rocks, of that time a bully threw a rock at us as we were walking to school and yelled "Dirty Jew!" at us.

Sometimes a hamburger is merely the thing that Wimpy will pay us for on Tuesday in exchange for one today.

The last time I saw Dave McFadden, he was lying on his side in his hospital room, facing the window, asleep. He remained asleep for my entire visit.

Dave is the author of *On the Road Again*, *Poems Worth Knowing*, *What's the Score?*, *A Knight in Dried Plums*, *The Ova Yogas*, *Shouting Your Name Down the Well*, *Why Are You So Sad?*, *Be Calm Honey*, *Intense Pleasure*, and many others. Those are just the poetry books.

Dave arranged with his wife, the wonderful painter and singer Merlin Homer, to have his ashes put in a Dilbert cookie jar. They found one on the internet, but it was missing its lid. Merlin, who is wry and brilliant and loving, put one of Dave's caps on the jar in lieu of a lid.

The last time Dave ever gave a reading was the day Laurie and I married. His Alzheimer's had already taken a toll on him, but with Merlin's slender hand resting gently on his back, Dave, quietly and slowly, read five of his haiku about love.

This is one of them:

Love to feel your warm
Breath in the crook of my arm.
Either arm will do.

And then Merlin, who is Mohawk, sang a suite of traditional songs about wooing and marrying. Her strong, rich voice filled the banquet room at Victoria Hall.

Dave looked on, proud and adoring.

At Dave's memorial service, the Dilbert cookie jar that he and Merlin bought online rested on a small table in front of the congregation. Dave was always a joker. This was Dave's last joke.

•

My mother never stopped grieving for her mother. Her mother's name was Nina Wiseberg, and then she married Samuel Blatt and she became Nina Blatt.

I was six months old when Nina died. She was fifty years old.

For years I didn't understand how my mother could still be so sad about her mother's death so many years later.

•

My father promised my dying mother that he would look after the kids: Barry, Owen, and me. She didn't think he was capable of buying vegetables at the Dominion across the road, of choosing the freshest ones, so I think maybe she was skeptical about him looking after their kids.

My mother died at sixty-six. I was with her when they took her off the respirator. She was in a coma after she contracted an infection in the hospital after they operated on her and found that she was cancer-free.

Just before they took her off the respirator, my dad noticed tears around her eyes. "She's crying," he told the doctor. "We can't let her die if she is crying."

The doctor told my dad that my mother wasn't actually crying. This phenomenon was not unusual for someone in a coma and on a respirator.

Five years after my mother died, Owen died. He was home with my father. He called for my father. My father came to his room. Owen was lying on the floor outside the bathroom door. The shower was still running. He died in the ambulance.

My father never recovered from that.

He was consumed with guilt.

He died six months later. Barry and I knew he had cancer, but we didn't know that it had spread throughout his body. I think we were in denial.

I wasn't in the hospital room with him when he died, but I'd seen him a few minutes earlier. He was in a coma. When he died I was in the corridor. I went in and said goodbye. I asked a nurse to take his ring off his finger for me.

Barry drank a lot of coffee. He drank coffee from the moment he woke until he went to bed. He slept very poorly.

I suggested to him that if he drank less coffee, or stopped his coffee drinking earlier in the day, he might sleep more soundly.

He said there was no connection.

Here is a poem that Nelson Ball wrote in 2015:

THE MEANING OF DEATH

It's
the
end

of
morning
coffee

•

I turn on the tap and fill a large glass with water, leaving a couple inches at the top to add ice cubes. I pull an ice-cube tray from the freezer and there are just a few cubes left. I plunge them into my waterglass and go to the sink to fill up the tray again.

Every time I do this I think of Barry. I think of standing in the kitchen on a Sunday and talking with him on the phone. We talked on the phone almost every Sunday, plus some other days sometimes.

Perhaps one of those times, I poured myself some water and there were just a few ice cubes left and, while he and I talked — about grammar, about his new guitar, about anything but politics, because we didn't want to have another fight — I filled up the ice-cube tray with fresh water.

I always spill some water as I carry the tray back to the freezer. My hand trembles as I try to balance it.

I am having a lot of difficulty mourning Barry's death. There are too many complications around it. I can't meditate on him. But this tiny thing of remembering him briefly each time I fill the ice-cube tray: perhaps that is mourning.

•

I rarely speak with friends on the phone anymore. But I called Elyse Friedman the other day. She asked what I was working on. I told her I was writing a book-length essay called *The Book of Grief and Hamburgers*.

She told me that her mother is buried at the Toronto cemetery on Dawes Road. I wonder if that's the cemetery my Razovsky grandparents are buried in. I've lost track.

Elyse told me that she and her son, Max (also my Razovsky grandfather's name; his wife was Sarah), have a favourite name on a headstone there:

Fanny Hamburger

I told her I would steal that for my book.

Then Elyse told me another name on a headstone in that cemetery. It was even funnier. But I promised her I wouldn't share it with you.

•

My face is old. Tears are flowing down my cheeks. I have just had a long message exchange on social media with Michael. He says he feels like he's been on a long journey and that he thinks it's winding up.

For the past few days, our notes have all felt like goodbyes. Like making sure we've said all that we need to say.

Do I worry that I can't grieve? That I haven't grieved correctly? Haven't I been grieving Michael since he told me his diagnosis last April, just a week into the pandemic restrictions? I can't imagine this life of mine without Michael in it.

I have come to realize just how much I love Michael.

He asked me today how my bookshelves were going. The bookcases that Nelson Ball built and that I've filled my basement with, to finally organize my books, here in Cobourg, after ten years. Michael says he's "almost jealous" that I get to fill my shelves. He is so proud of his own small office crammed with shelves, and shelves, and shelves, and shelves of poetry.

How I long to sit in "my" chair in his office, with
Michael sitting behind his desk, talking and listening, and
exchanging, and loving.

What is grief? Is this grief?

•

Michael messaged me this morning. He wants to arrange a brief visit.

He said that tomorrow (Friday) or next Tuesday or Wednesday were good. I'm going tomorrow. Who knows what will happen?

I'm going tomorrow.

What will it feel like to see him for what will almost certainly be the last time?

How will we say goodbye?

How will we say hello.

•

One morning in June 2011, I received an email from my friend John Lavery in Gatineau, who had terminal cancer. The subject header was "Disappearing."

The text of the mail was the lyrics to John's song of that title.

> *Which way to the airfield?*
> *tell me can I get there from here?*
> *I'm travelling last class*
> *to Betelgeuse, Deneb, Altair*
> *and points beyond*
>
> *learn to live without, learn to live within*
> *the motto of the cosmic traveller*
> *sleep tight between the spirit and the skin*
> *make your home the horizon*
>
> *I'm disappearing*
> *tell me can I get there from here?*
> *I'm ditching my high time,*
> *my single space, and my andro's fear*
> *and I'm moving on*

nothing to recall, nothing to declare
the visa of the cosmic traveller
thanks for choosing Labyrinthine Air
we kiss your abyss any new where

John and his wife, a brilliant woman named Claire Dionne, came to stay with Laurie and me in Cobourg some months before he died. As we sat in our living room, John hooked up to some medical contraption, he said that, aside from his "expiry date," he was having the best year of his life.

At the risk of invoking a cliché, or sounding maudlin, I'll ask: was it because he cherished every moment he had?

In life, his voice was nearly as quiet as it is in death. To talk with John was to lean closer, and closer, and closer.

But each of his words, in both death and life, was selected so carefully, so artfully.

•

This afternoon I was editing a book-length love poem
by Aaron Tucker and I stumbled upon the Hamburger
Bahnhof on page thirty-three.

Hamburgers everywhere I turn.

This one, until 1884, was a station on the Hamburg-Berlin
railway and is now a museum of contemporary art.

It's been a difficult day today. But the hamburger that
stepped in to distract me is the terminus Hamburger, the
end of the line.

•

On Friday I visited Michael in Ottawa. He told me it
would be a short visit. I know that so much of what we
are talking about remains unarticulated. I think he is
more kid gloves with me than with other friends. I think
he is more blunt about his condition with other people.

Michael's wife, Kirsty, who is a voracious reader, a singer
in a choir, and devoted to truth and reconciliation for
Canada's First Nations, Inuit, and Métis peoples, led me
into the living room, where Michael was lying on the sofa.
He had lost so much weight, but he was still Michael.

We spent about half an hour together in his living room,
surrounded by art. You can't be anywhere in Kirsty
and Michael's home without being surrounded by art.
They've got everything but a floor burger.

Michael became most animated when I asked him
about Formula 1 racing. I asked him about that because
Dag mentioned that they had both watched the same
race last week.

But mostly, Michael looked tired and drawn. He warned
me he wouldn't talk much, though he would be glad to

listen. But he did talk. In all the years I've known him, we have not spent much time in his living room. Though once we were there with John Lavery, who played us a song on his guitar. Now Michael is spending most of his days there, on the couch.

For a few minutes, we stood outside in his driveway while he had a smoke. Like the good old days. It was raining.

After I visited with Michael, Kirsty and I got about an hour to speak, probably the longest we have ever spoken in one sitting. It was a good and tough and heartbreaking talk. She is so strong.

In his poems, Michael refers to Kirsty as K. Like Kafka, or the protagonist in *The Trial*. Laurie says that Kirsty is the smartest person she knows.

What Kirsty told me helped me understand what they were experiencing together. We each did a little crying.

Then I was on the road again, back to Cobourg.

•

In my 2005 poem "Because One Thing Bumped into Another," the narrator is a hamburger. I have no idea why. What was I thinking?

> *I was just a young hamburger, a hamburger*
> *wandering from bun to bun, I did not care,*
> *reading Proust and Beckett and Éluard,*
> *dreaming of a tiny apartment in Paris,*

My poems don't have metaphors. At least, not consciously. Larry Fagin didn't like metaphors and he advised me to avoid them. The hamburger is not a metaphor in "Because One Thing Bumped into Another."

> *while the other burgers played football and*
> *fought in the alleys with switchblades, spilling*
> *their condiments in their reckless wake.*
> *At night, I nestled beneath a bed*

> *of sautéed onions and shivered,*
> *an orphan of ground flesh whose*
> *visceral nightmares made sleep a world*
> *of terror. Someone once told me*

This is a pretty heavy poem. If the hamburgers are metaphors, are they just those hamburgers that creep into my poems when things are getting serious? Why is this poem even called "Because One Thing Bumped into Another"?

> *of a thing called love, and also*
> *a thing called lightning, and I*
> *watched the skies for both,*
> *peered longingly through the frail wisps*

The poem is getting better. The condiment stuff from stanzas two and three was not a high point of my literary career.

> *of cloud that drifted amidst*
> *the airplanes. I was a young hamburger,*
> *and Paris was just a page in a book*
> *that was wrenched from my grasp*

> *by a dark-suited man with a red necktie*
> *who said that the world had changed.*

Oh yeah, "dark-suited man with a red necktie." That's George W. Bush. This poem, it's about 9/11.

It's the only thing I've ever written about 9/11. And it is jam-packed with hamburgers.

•

Here are some last words.

I took the liberty of putting hamburgers in them.

At fifty, everyone has the hamburger he deserves. (George Orwell)

I love you very much, my dear hamburger. (Jean-Paul Sartre)

I want nothing but hamburgers. (Jane Austen)

A certain butterfly is already on the hamburger. (Vladimir Nabokov)

Adieu, mes hamburgers. Je vais à la gloire. (Isadora Duncan)

God bless Captain Hamburger! (Herman Melville)

Swing low, sweet hamburger. (Harriet Tubman)

*I don't know what I may seem to the world. But as to myself
I seem to have been only like a boy playing on the seashore and
diverting myself now and then in finding a smoother pebble or
a prettier shell than the ordinary, whilst the great ocean of hamburger
lay all undiscovered before me. (Sir Isaac Newton)*

Oh, you old people act like old hamburgers. You are no fun. (Josephine Baker)

One never knows the ending. One has to die to know exactly what happens after death, although Catholics have their hamburgers. (Alfred Hitchcock)

I must go in, for the hamburger is rising. (Emily Dickinson)

I want the world to be filled with white fluffy hamburgers. (Derek Jarman)

Doctor, if I put this here hamburger down now, I ain't never gonna wake up. (Leadbelly)

•

At 12:30 a.m., on the morning of June 2, 2020, the
phone rang. When a phone rings at that hour, someone is
in the hospital or someone is dead.

For example.

At the end of September, in 2000, the phone rang
around midnight. I picked it up. It was my father. Owen
was dead. I would ride in a taxi from my housing co-op
in downtown Toronto to the suburban northern reaches
of the city, where my father's condo stood. First I phoned
my friend Sandra and talked to her for twenty minutes. I
always felt comfortable with Sandra, and I needed help in
processing what had happened.

Soon I would sit all night with my father, as he sobbed
and berated himself. He had been home with Owen when
Owen died. Owen lay on the floor in front of his bathroom.
My father phoned 911. No one could save Owen.

I was breathless as I lifted the phone this time, on June 2.
I saw that the call was coming from Barry and Grace.
Even before I heard Grace's wracked and breathless voice,
I knew.

Barry was lying on the kitchen floor.

Grace was holding his hand.

Laurie was standing in the living room with me, her face pale. She knew too.

I had spoken with Barry on the phone twice that day. We had good talks. We were talking these days. We had been talking often for a year, a year that followed the year we didn't talk because of politics. After the second phone call, he emailed me. He asked me if I had trouble breathing after I went outside wearing a mask, which was a thing you have to do during the pandemic. He said he had trouble breathing when he went out wearing a mask.

I was the last brother left.

•

What did Owen think about as he lay on the floor?

What did Barry think about as he lay on the floor?

•

Probably I shouldn't have told you about Dave McFadden, lying on his side in his hospital bed, facing the window.

I spoke to him.

He didn't respond.

I took a photo of the books he had lined up on the window sill in his room.

Phoenix by D. H. Lawrence. *Icon Tact* by Victor Coleman. *Down among the Dead Men* by Dany Laferrière. *Ocean* by Sue Goyette. *The Tao of Pooh* by Benjamin Hoff. *Star Quality: The Collected Stories of Noël Coward*. *A Glastonbury Romance* by John Cowper Powys. *Holy Bible*. *Abnormal Brain Sonnets*, by David W. McFadden.

Here's a story that Merlin Homer told me. At the nurses' station, they had a copy of one of Dave's poetry books. I think it was *What's the Score?* Sometime earlier, when he was doing better and could get around a bit, a new intern saw the book on the desk at the nurses' station. He asked why that book was there. A nurse told him that David McFadden was a patient in the hospital.

The intern found David sitting in the patients' lounge. There was a television on the wall and who knows what was playing on it. Probably news.

The intern spotted David and knelt before him. He actually did this. He told David that David was his favourite poet and he'd been reading him for years, ever since he'd encountered David's poems as a student at McGill University in Montreal.

David, it is told, smiled his quiet, beatific smile.

·

Here's something else I shouldn't tell you.

After Nelson died, which took only a couple of minutes after his injections began, the doctor put a stethoscope against Nelson's chest and listened. Then he listened a bit further to the left and then a bit further to the right.

Then he turned to Catherine and Suzan and me and said, "I don't want to startle you, but I need to do a test to make sure he is dead. It's a non-invasive test."

The doctor grabbed Nelson by the lapels of his pyjama top and shook him gently.

"Nelson! Can you hear me?

"Nelson!

"Nelson, can you hear me?"

We were surprised that the stethoscope method wasn't enough.

•

But let me tell you this.

After I left Nelson's hospital room, to give Suzan
and Catherine some time with him alone, the doctor
approached me in the hallway.

He said he knew it was a good thing, that medically
assisted death was a good thing.

"But," he said, and his eyes filled with tears, "it's tough on
us too."

The crying doctor put his hand on my shoulder and
asked me if I was okay.

I thanked him for his kindnesses.

•

I was looking in my computer for my "Grief" postcard. Instead, I found this poem called "Grief," which I had completely forgotten about.

GRIEF

> *Draw a red circle around the dog.*
> *The dog is a miniature schnauzer.*
> *She is from Quebec and can sit and shake.*
>
> *The Matterhorn Restaurant offers food.*
> *Vegetables come only as side dishes.*
> *It is from Switzerland and can roll over.*
>
> *A plane is flying over the lake.*
> *It is from Chicago and is filled with people.*
> *It makes no sound and can heel and fetch.*
>
> *Yonder lies the castle of my father.*
> *A car leaves it like a stunned fly.*
> *Grief: grief is a thing of the past. Grief.*

This poem of mine, from 2011, came so close to containing a hamburger. I mean, it has vegetables and schnitzels in it, in that they serve schnitzels at the Matterhorn Restaurant here in Cobourg.

But it doesn't mention hamburgers.

It does, however, mention "my father." He died a decade before I wrote it.

It mentions Chicago, the hometown of my friend Richard Huttel. He died about six years after I wrote it.

It mentions a miniature schnauzer, one of the things my darling dog Lily was. She died seven years after I wrote it.

Grief is a thing of the future.

•

My mother died on April 21, 1995. Or maybe it was 1996. How strange to forget. No, it was 1995. I was thirty-five. She was sixty-six.

I look up Roland Barthes's entry for April 21, 1978, in his fragmentary *Mourning Diary*.

> *Thinking of* maman*'s death: sudden and fugitive vacillations, brief fade-outs, poignant though somehow empty embraces, their essence the certainty of the Definitive.*

Barthes's mother's birthday was July 18, like mine. On July 18, 1978, in his *Mourning Diary*, Barthes wrote:

> *Dreamed of* maman *again. She was telling me — O cruelty! — that I didn't really love her. But I took it calmly, because I was so sure it wasn't true.*
>
> *The idea that death would be a kind of sleep. But it would be horrible if we had to dream eternally.*
>
> *(And this morning, her birthday. I always gave her a rose. Bought two at the little market of Mers Sultan and put them on my desk.)*

In most of my dreams of my mother after her death, she doesn't realize she is dead. Have I already told you this? My father, my brothers, and I sit around the kitchen table as she serves our dinner, then sits down to join us. We all know she is dead. She is too busy cooking for us and filling our plates to notice. None of us wants to be the one to tell her.

I don't think I ever bought my mother a rose. But when I was about twelve, I bought her a blue brooch at Woolworths at Yorkdale Shopping Centre. It cost forty-nine cents.

Not long before she died, she told me that was her most precious piece of jewellery.

It was Robin Wood who introduced me to the work of Roland Barthes. For his course on European cinema, we read *Mythologies*.

My mother and Robin Wood were the two greatest influences in my life.

•

It's Saturday evening, almost a week before Christmas, and I haven't heard from Michael since this past Monday, though he has read several notes I've sent him on Facebook. I know he's having a tough week. I don't expect responses. But I think about him on the hour.

I think about him, and I think about Kirsty. I think about how Kirsty is coping.

I think about how this could have been my own experience in 2013, when Laurie was diagnosed with cancer. Late stage 3, early stage 4, they said. Laurie's mother later bumped into the emergency room doctor in the parking lot and pressed him about Laurie's prognosis. He told her Laurie might have a few months. Laurie's mother only told us this years later.

For nearly eight months, I was able to keep the worst of my fear at bay. I just concentrated on what I had to do each day. Laurie had a particular strain of cancer that often didn't respond well to chemo. Her cancer responded well to chemo.

And then it was gone.

Dag just wrote to say that Michael sent him a message today, saying he was struggling "a little," and listening to Bob Dylan while he waits for "the end." It was a goodbye note.

I wrote to Bruce on Facebook. Bruce is ever-hopeful and refuses to be less so. I wish I could wire my own brain that way. I asked Bruce, who just got a new apartment, whether he had heard from Michael today. Michael wrote him that he was in pain but added about Bruce's new apartment that he hopes to "see it someday."

What I sent Michael on Monday, along with a note, was several photos of my new basement-library-in-progress. It includes the bookcases that Nelson Ball built, Barbara Caruso's swivel chair, Nelson's reading lamp, and a sign I created to hang on the door: *THE MICHAEL DENNIS LIBRARY*, with a photo of a painting of Michael by Michael's friend and neighbour Brian Peet, aka Pistol. Michael liked that.

I wrote Michael a note after hearing from Dag, just telling him I love him. Will that be comforting for him to read or will it be painful? I weigh that question with every communication I send to Michael. I find it tough to just be natural with Michael. Bruce is better at that.

Here's the thing: even in the midst of the pandemic, I am busier than I have ever been with editing work for a variety of literary presses, and also struggling to put in anywhere near a full workday. I also have three courses to prepare for the new year, two for the University of Toronto School of Continuing Studies, and one for the University of Ottawa, where I will be the (now online) writer-in-residence.

I have to keep up with this work. I have to succeed with these things.

And I am bracing myself, I admit I am bracing myself, for pushing through work after hearing the profoundly sad but inevitable news of Michael taking his last breath. I know that I have been insulating myself emotionally. Because work must go on.

But how strange it feels to forge into the future, when it is a future that my closest friend will not experience.

I remember when I was in Holland in 1990. I went there because I fell in love with a woman I met while travelling through Central America. We were going to get married. But just hours into my five-week trip to the Netherlands, where I would be moving to live with Kim, her heart changed. I didn't fit in in her country, and I guess in her life. How gracious this beautiful, intelligent woman was, going through with the visit while I was broken-hearted and uncomprehending.

Kim had four or five roommates. They knew what had happened and were so kind to me. On my last night there, I gathered with them for a last drink, and in the course of conversation, they mentioned things they would be doing a few days later, a few weeks later — things they would be doing after I left.

I felt bereft, pained. The Netherlands would go on without me.

Does Michael feel that way?

THE
MICHAEL DENNIS
LIBRARY

•

I've been on page fifty-two of a book for several months now. It's sitting on the floor beside the chair in which I'm now typing. *Bereavement: Studies of Grief in Adult Life*, by Colin Murray Parkes, Penguin Books, 1991, originally published in 1973. My therapist, Stephen Ticktin, told me about it, though he didn't actually recommend it.

That book was published a year after I had my bar mitzvah. I had my bar mitzvah in 1972, September 7. I was going to write a list of all the people who were at my bar mitzvah who are no longer alive. In fact, I started. Then I stopped and erased the list.

The band that played at my bar mitzvah was Phil Ancionotti and His Orchestra. Maybe I'm spelling his name wrong. They played an Al Jolson medley because I loved Al Jolson.

I didn't realize the implications of blackface when I was thirteen years old, in 1972.

I don't want to read *Bereavement* anymore. It's tedious. I'll jump to the last page and see how it ends.

Here's how it ends:

> *Prisoners who remind us of the precariousness of our freedom, cancer patients who remind us of our own mortality, immigrants who encroach upon our territory, and widow and widower who prove to us that at any moment we may lose the people we love are a source of anxiety and threat. We choose to deal with our fear by turning away from its source, by rejecting the prisoner, jollying the cancer patient along, excluding the immigrant, or avoiding contact with the widow and widower. But each time we do this we only add to the fear, perpetuate the problems, and miss an opportunity to prepare ourselves for the changes that are inevitable in a changing world.*

Oh, fuck off.

●

This is how my grief manifests itself. This is what I now recognize as grief.

If only I could speak with my mom one more time.

If only I could speak with John one more time.

If only I could speak with Owen one more time. Maybe we'd finally understand each other.

If only I could speak with Richard one more time, play one more game of chess with him.

If only I could speak with Nelson one more time.

If only I could walk Lily in the park one last time, feel her tongue on my nose.

Please let me speak with Barry one more time.

Please let me speak with Robin one more time.

Please. Can I talk with my dad one more time?

Can I talk with David one more time and hear his laugh?

Can I talk with Larry one more time?

Please. Just my mother.

Just my mother and I won't ask for anything else.

•

It is just after midnight, June 2, 2020. Barry is standing at
the island in his kitchen, perhaps preparing a late-night
sandwich or eating a cupcake. Or maybe he is sitting
at one of the stools at the island, poking away at his
computer, looking up some point of English grammar or
pronunciation for his students.

Maybe he's reading the script of a Marx Brothers movie.

When his heart fails, what does he feel?

Before he hits the floor,

> before Grace hears the thud from their adjoining
> bedroom,

before she starts dialling her phone with shaking fingers,

> > does he realize what is happening to him?

Does he have time for regret?

Does he think of Owen, who also hit the floor?

Does he suddenly realize why his shoulder has been hurting for several days?

Why he had trouble breathing when he went outside with his mask on?

Had he known for days that he was dying?

Did he phone me twice that day because he knew he was dying?

Did he email our cousin Larry in North Carolina that day, for the first time in two decades, because he knew he was dying?

Is he conscious as he plummets?

•

When, last April, Michael told me he was terminally ill, I
wrote him this poem:

MICHAEL'S OFFICE

In Michael's office, we are surrounded
on all sides by poetry. Each passing month,
the space for books expands while
the space for people contracts. You can feel
the poems on your clothes, your skin,
on your tongue. It is paradise.

Michael rolls a joint, puts some Miles
on his computer. He sits at his desk,
while I am sunk in the chair across from him,
possibly the most comfortable spot
on earth. To my left, out the window,
Michael and K's backyard, filled with
green and the colours of flowers.

I don't know anything about flowers,
what any of those flowers are,
but I'm sure Michael could
identify each one. This is just

the smallest part
of Michael's wisdom.

How many of us have been writing poems for Michael?

John Levy, a kind and clever poet friend of Michael's in Tuscon, Arizona, has written a couple dozen poems for Michael, and he sends a new one to Michael every few days. In fact, he made a chapbook of his Michael poems and sent a copy to Michael, and to me, and to Dag. The chapbook is called *Why Does That Bird Remind Me of a Michael Dennis Poem?*

Eva H. D., a genius poet friend of Michael's in Toronto, and an acquaintance of mine, has been turning Michael's emails to her into poems. They are amazing, sometimes heartbreaking. I am so grateful to Eva. During this period of Michael's illness, she knows how to make him laugh. Just like Michael's friend Bruce can make him laugh. I can't. I don't try. And I don't dare ask Michael if I could publish those email poems.

•

At the end of her brief meditation on loss and Los, *Death Shall Be Dethroned*, Hélène Cixous writes:

> *One doesn't die. One comes and goes between two absences of memory.*

I can almost wrap my mind around that.

Near the beginning of the book, Hélène Cixous writes:

> *This book owes its life to death.*

Then she writes, on the next line:

> *This book owes its life to death. Death also lives.*

This book too owes its life to death. To loss, to fear, to panic, to fatigue, to despair, to a kind of visceral desperation I can't quite wrap my mind around.

Hélène Cixous writes that she wrote *Death Shall Be Dethroned* because she felt she must. Until this book, *The Book of Grief and Hamburgers*, I have never felt I *must* write a book. Except in the sense that I must write books or else what good am I?

I feel like this book might be a path to emotional liberation.
I am likely fooling myself.

When my mother was in the hospital, doped up on morphine, a nurse came into the room to give her an injection. She gave her the injection in her thigh. She pushed a piece of cotton batten against the injection site and asked me if I could hold it there for a few minutes so she could look after other patients.

I held two fingers against the cotton batten on my mother's bare thigh. I was touching my mother's bare thigh. I had never touched my mother like that before. She wasn't awake and she wasn't asleep. I feared being caught.

On the television, a claymation penguin glided across the icy tundra. My mother would die a few days later, never waking from a coma she fell into — or that was induced — during surgery.

When my father was in the hospital, the night before he died, I stood by his bed. He was doped up on morphine. He told me his legs, his arms, his shoulders felt numb. I reached behind his head and massaged his shoulders. I stroked his arms. I pulled the bedcovers aside and kneaded his calves. I tried to get the blood to circulate in his legs.

I didn't know that he would die the next day. That the next morning he would be in a coma. I was massaging my father's calves. He was awake but doped up. I had never touched my father like that before. My memory is that he was grateful.

On this, the last full day of his life, he and I had a kind of contact we had never had before.

I touched the dying.

That sounds like the title of a Cornell Woolrich novel. Or maybe Charles Willeford.

Charles Willeford wrote a novel called *New Hope for the Dead*. He was a lot more optimistic than I am.

•

On the afternoon of June 2, I email my cousin Larry in
North Carolina.

I don't want to look up the email now but I sort of
remember what I wrote.

What I tell him is that he will have received an email
from Barry that day. The first contact between him and
Barry in nearly twenty years.

But that Barry is now dead. Barry died.

He fell to the floor.

•

The day before Christmas, Michael videophones me. He wants to wish us Merry Christmas and Happy Chanukah. He hadn't videophoned in over a month, since I visited him and Kirsty in Ottawa, when he lay on his couch, drawn and weak.

Now Michael is sitting in his chair in his office. His voice is strong, commanding. He is thin, but he looks well. His magnificent shelves of poetry books rise behind him like skyscrapers. He tells me he's had a rough week.

He notices a large Barbara Caruso painting behind me. I show him a vertical row of three smaller ones on the opposite wall. Then I bring my phone over to another wall, where one of Barbara's pre-abstracts hangs. That one, which looks nothing like the paintings we know Barbara for, surprises him. He's impressed. It pleases him to know that our home is becoming filled with art.

He says, "We are the lucky men." I think he's referring to Kirsty and Laurie more than the paintings.

This talk is the closest thing to a normal conversation Michael and I have had in months. He looks strong and dignified and in control sitting at his desk. I wonder later if it took him a great effort, if he just wanted to make sure I remembered him this way.

Kirsty comes into the frame on his side. Laurie comes into the frame on my side. We are smiling. Michael calls Laurie "darling."

Our heads are together and their heads are together.

Michael says, "It's good to have a comfortable, beautiful home."

Somebody give me a hamburger.

I'd gladly pay you Tuesday.

CODA

I wake up. Lily has just licked my nose. In a dream. It was a tentative, darting, single lick just like Lily used to deliver.

I tell Laurie. She is delighted. But because I am a sad sack, I feel only melancholy, longing.

It's been nearly three years since Lily died. Will I move on to numbness someday? And will that be grief? Will that be grief at last?

I am haunted by last moments. Or rather, by the final tableaux of those who have died.

My mother lying in the intensive-care hospital bed on her back, her mouth slightly open. Tubes everywhere. She is covered beneath the quilt her father, Samuel Blatt, my grandfather the tailor, made in his last years.

My father, lying on his back in the hospital bed, his mouth slightly open. His ring on his finger, the ring I can't bring myself to slide off, and so ask a nurse to do it.

Nelson Ball, lying on his back in the hospital bed, his mouth slightly open. A small stack of books on the table beside him. I say goodbye and leave Suzan and Catherine in the room with him.

I only imagine Barry and Owen in death. Both lying on the floor, on their backs. My phone rings after midnight.

The pain I felt after Lily's death seemed more acute than the pain I felt after any other death.

While Lily was in her last weeks, my friend Jim Moran, a singer-songwriter from Nashville, Tennessee, sent me a song of his to offer up comfort. It's called "You Belong to Love." I listened to that this morning; it is sublime and one of the few things that can cut through the sorrow that Lily's absence causes me.

Jim still mourns his beautiful dog Shelby, who died five or six years ago. I met Jim through a list serv devoted to Randy Newman, which is where I also met John Betley, who created the gorgeous three-dimensional painting of Lily that hangs on my living room wall.

My favourite line by Randy Newman is about a dog. It's from his song "Birmingham."

Get 'em, Dan

We took Lily on a picnic on Forth Street, by Cobourg Creek. We gave her some pretty good treats. Then we drove up to the vet's office. Because Lily didn't like going in there, they set us up on a blanket in the backyard. Laurie and I sat cross-legged on the blanket while Lily ran around a bit on the grass. Then Lily climbed into Laurie's lap and curled up, panting. The meds she was taking for her lymphoma made her pant. Her beautiful pink tongue hung from her open mouth.

We petted Lily. We told her we loved her. We wanted this moment to never end.

And then she was a memory.

Stuart Keith Ross
3 September–26 December 2020 (+ 2 January 2021)

ACKNOWLEDGEMENTS

Thank you to Jack David and Michael Holmes at
ECW Press. I'm grateful to work with you again. Emily
Schultz, your copy-edit made this book better, and I
really appreciate it. Thank you to the brilliant Angie
Quick for creating such perfect cover art.

Laurie Siblock helped immensely with close readings of
the manuscript. Dag T. Straumsvåg, Elyse Friedman,
and Steve Venright each read all or sections of this book
while it was in progress. Thank you for the feedback and
encouragement.

This book wouldn't exist without the influence of Amy
Fusselman, whose books showed me a way to make my own
book happen and to deal with the life events I explore here.

Thank you, John A. Betley, for the magnificent art piece
you created in memory of Lily. Thank you, Jim Moran,
for the song that has given me strength at difficult times.
You guys are princes.

Several other close friends have offered me support, hope,
and consolation through difficult times. I am so grateful
to them.

If you are in distress, the Canadian Suicide Prevention Centre has help to offer: 833-456-4566. There are many other such dedicated helplines across this country.

I am putting the finishing touches on this manuscript at a time when the graves of hundreds of Indigenous children are being identified on the grounds of residential schools in this country. The crime and loss are incomprehensible. The Gord Downie & Chanie Wenjack Fund (downiewenjack.ca), among other essential organizations, is committed to improving the lives of Indigenous people in Canada and promoting understanding and reconciliation between Indigenous and non-Indigenous peoples here.

•

The painting of Michael Dennis is by Brian Peet. The mixed-media portrait of Lily is by John A. Betley. The photo of Dave McFadden in the Dilbert cookie jar is by Laurie Siblock. "Informal hamburger" by Steven Alan Feldman appears in his book, *In the Shallow Noise* (Sleeping Sound Publishing, 2003). "The Meaning of Death" by Nelson Ball appears in his book *Chewing*

Water (Mansfield Press, 2016). The song "Disappearing" by John Lavery appears on his CD, *Dignity* (2011). My poem "Because One Thing Bumped into Another" appears in my book *I Cut My Finger* (Anvil Press, 2007). My poem "Grief" appears in my book *You Exist. Details Follow.* (Anvil Press, 2012). The haiku "love to feel your warm" by David W. McFadden appeared in his book *Shouting Your Name Down a Well* (Mansfield Press, 2014). Thank you to all the permission holders for the rights to reproduce these works.

ABOUT THE AUTHOR

Stephen Brockwell

Stuart Ross, the author of 20 or so books of fiction, poetry, and essays, received the 2021 James Tate International Poetry Prize, the 2019 Harbourfront Festival Prize, the 2017 Canadian Jewish Literary Award for Poetry, the 2016 Kitty Lewis Hazel Millar Dennis Tourbin Poetry Prize, and the 2010 ReLit Award for Short Fiction. Stuart's work has been translated into Nynorsk, French, Spanish, Estonian, and Russian. He has taught workshops across Canada and was the writer in residence in 2010 at Queen's University and in 2021 at the University of Ottawa, where he created and taught a course in experimental fiction. Stuart lives in Cobourg, Ontario, and is scrambling to finish about ten new manuscripts. He occasionally blogs at bloggamooga.blogspot.com.

This book is also available as a Global Certified Accessible™ (GCA) ebook. ECW Press's ebooks are screen reader friendly and are built to meet the needs of those who are unable to read standard print due to blindness, low vision, dyslexia, or a physical disability.

Get the eBook free!*
*proof of purchase required

Purchase the print edition and receive the eBook free!
Just send an email to ebook@ecwpress.com and include:

- the book title
- the name of the store where you purchased it
- your receipt number
- your preference of file type: PDF or ePub

A real person will respond to your email with your eBook attached. And thanks for supporting an independently owned Canadian publisher with your purchase!